Wants Versus Needs

Food and Drink

Linda Staniford

heinemann
raintree

To contact Capstone Global Library, please call 800-747-4992, or visit our web site www.capstonepub.com

Edited by Linda Staniford and Shelly Lyons
Designed by Philippa Jenkins
Original illustrations © Capstone Global Library Ltd 2014
Picture research by Tracy Cummins
Production by Helen McCreath
Originated by Capstone Global Library Ltd
Printed and bound in China by Leo Paper Group

18 17 16 15 14
10 9 8 7 6 5 4 3 2 1

Library of Congress Cataloging-in-Publication Data
Staniford, Linda.
 Food and drink / Linda Staniford.
    pages cm.—(Wants vs. needs)
 Includes bibliographical references and index.
  ISBN 978-1-4846-0943-9 (hb)—ISBN 978-1-4846-0948-4 (pb)—ISBN 978-1-4846-0958-3 (ebook) 1. Nutrition—Juvenile literature. 2. Food—Psychological aspects—Juvenile literature. 3. Need (Psychology)—Juvenile literature. I. Title.

 TX355.S73 2015
 363.8—dc23   2014015023

This book has been officially leveled by using the F&P Text Level Gradient™ Leveling System.

Acknowledgments
We would like to thank the following for permission to reproduce photographs: Capstone Press: Karon Dubke, 8, 17, 22 Bottom, 23C, Philippa Jenkins, Cover Left, Design Elements; Getty Images: Image Source, 18; Shutterstock: Christian Draghici, 7, Fanfo, 9, Gladskikh Tatiana, 19, Hurst Photo, 10, 23D, Jacek Chabraszewski, 6, Kzenon, 12, 23B, lightwavemedia, 20, M. Unal Ozmen, 16, Maks Narodenko, 1, Cover Right, Marc Dietrich, 14, Monkey Business Images, 13, 15, 21, 23E, Back Cover, Nitr, 22 Top, Ruth Black, 11, Tatyana Vyc, 4, 23A, Thomas M Perkins, 5.

Every effort has been made to contact copyright holders of material reproduced in this book. Any omissions will be rectified in subsequent printings if notice is given to the publisher.

Disclaimer
All the Internet addresses (URLs) given in this book were valid at the time of going to press. However, due to the dynamic nature of the Internet, some addresses may have changed, or sites may have changed or ceased to exist since publication. While the author and publisher regret any inconvenience this may cause readers, no responsibility for any such changes can be accepted by either the author or the publisher.

Contents

Some words are shown in bold, **like this**. You
can find them in the glossary on page 23.

What Are Needs and Wants?

Needs are things we cannot live without. We need food and drink for **energy** and to keep our bodies working properly.

Wants are things we would like to have.
Some kinds of food and drink are wants.
Chocolate is a food you may want but
do not need.

What Foods Do We Need to Eat?

We need to eat **healthy** foods that will make us grow strong and give us **energy**. This will help keep our bodies working well.

Too much of the wrong food is not good for you. You may want a hamburger and fries, but that is not a healthy meal!

What Foods Will Make Us Grow?

Our bodies need **protein** to grow.
Protein is in foods like meat, fish, nuts,
eggs and beans. You need to eat some
protein each day.

We may want to eat fried meat or fish.
But fried food is not **healthy**.

What Foods Will Give Us Energy?

We need to eat starchy foods that give us **energy**. Bread, rice, and pasta all have **starch**. You need to eat some of these things each day.

Cakes and cookies give us lots of energy. But this energy comes from sugar and fat. Too much sugar and fat is bad for us.

What Foods Will Keep Us Healthy?

We need to eat foods that keep us looking and feeling **healthy**. Fruits and vegetables help to do this. You need to eat different kinds of fruits and vegetables each day.

Fruits and vegetables have **vitamins**. Our bodies need vitamins to stay healthy.

What Can We Eat Between Meals?

You may want to eat snacks such as chips. These taste good, but you should not eat them too often. They have a lot of fat, which is bad for your heart.

If you feel hungry between meals, you should choose a **healthy** snack. You could eat some vegetable sticks or nuts.

Is Sugar Bad for Us?

Ice cream, candy, and chocolate taste good, but they are sugary. Sugar is bad for your teeth and your body.

Instead of sweets, you could eat some fruit. Fruit has some sugar, but it also has **vitamins**, which your body needs.

What Can We Drink?

You might want to try drinks that are sweet and bubbly. But these drinks often have a lot of sugar in them. Fruit juice has a lot of sugar, too.

If you are thirsty, the best drink is water. You need to drink plenty of water each day. Water satisfies your thirst and keeps you **healthy**.

Can We Have Some of the Foods That Are Bad for Us?

You can eat some chips, cake, and ice cream. But you should not eat these foods too often.

You need to make sure that you eat
healthy foods every day.

Quiz

Which of these meals do you want, and which do you need?

Picture Glossary

 **energy** the power to be active

 **healthy** being fit and well

 **protein** food that makes your body grow

 **starch** one type of food that gives you energy

 **vitamin** substance found in foods such as fruits and vegetables that helps keep your body healthy

Index

Note to Parents and Teachers

Reading nonfiction texts for information is an important part of a child's literary development. Readers can be encouraged to ask simple questions and then use the text to find the answers. Each chapter in this book begins with a question. Read the questions together. Look at the pictures. Talk about what the answer might be. Then, read the text to find out if your predictions were correct. To develop readers' inquiry skills, encourage them to think of other questions they might ask about the topic. Discuss where you could find the answers. Assist children in using the contents page, picture glossary, and index to practice research skills and new vocabulary words.